D1489611

THREAT TO THE SPOTTED OWL

Carol Parenzan Smalley

Mitchell Lane
PUBLISHERS

P.O. Box 196
Hockessin, Delaware 19707
Visit us on the web: www.mitchelllane.com
Comments? email us: mitchelllane@mitchelllane.com

Printing   1   2   3   4   5   6   7   8   9

A Robbie Reader/On the Verge of Extinction: Crisis in the Environment

Frogs in Danger
Polar Bears on the Hudson Bay
The Snows of Kilimanjaro
Threat to Ancient Egyptian Treasures
Threat to Haiti
Threat to the Bengal Tiger

Threat to the Giant Panda
Threat to the Leatherback Turtle
Threat to the Monarch Butterfly
Threat to the Spotted Owl
Threat to the Whooping Crane
Threat to the Yangtze River Dolphin

Library of Congress Cataloging-in-Publication Data
Smalley, Carol Parenzan, 1960–
  Threat to the spotted owl / by Carol Parenzan Smalley.
    p. cm. — (A Robbie reader. On the verge of extinction)
  Includes bibliographical references.
  ISBN 978-1-58415-687-1 (library bound : alk. paper)
  1. Northern spotted owl—Juvenile literature. 2. Endangered species—Juvenile literature. I. Title.
  QL696.S83S56 2009
  333.95'897—dc22

                                                              2008020889

ABOUT THE AUTHOR: Carol Parenzan Smalley lives in a log cabin in the Adirondack Mountains of upstate New York with her husband, Reid, her daughter, Elise, and their two Siamese cats, Junie B. and Amber Brown. Elise named the felines for two of her favorite children's book characters. Carol enjoys hiking in the woods and looking and listening for critters of the North Country—but there are no spotted owls in the Adirondack Mountains. She often takes photographs of her hiking adventures to share with family and friends. She has an environmental engineering degree from The Pennsylvania State University, and she enjoys sharing her love of nature with young readers. This is her fourth book for Mitchell Lane Publishers.

SPECIAL THANKS to biologist and photographer Jared Hobbs of British Columbia for his insight and photographs. Also to R. J. Gutiérrez for sharing his knowledge and passion for spotted owls with the author.

PHOTO CREDITS: Cover, pp. 1, 3, 4, 8, 10, 11, 12, 14, 15, 16, 19, 20, 21, 23 and background photos—Jared Hobbs (www.hobbsphotos.com); p. 7—South Okanagan Rehab Centre for Owls; p. 22—Sharon Beck; p. 24—Gerard Burkhart/Getty Images.

TABLE OF CONTENTS

Words in **bold** type can be found in the glossary.

Today, there are very few spotted owls living in the ancient forests of the world. To help spotted owls survive, laws have been passed to protect the bird. Humans cannot hunt or harm the owl in some parts of its range.

STOP THE TRUCK!

In October 2006, workers witnessed an unusual sight. While driving through Manning Park in southern British Columbia in Canada, they saw an owl in the middle of the road. It wasn't just any owl, though. It was a spotted owl—a rare and **endangered** (en-DAYN-jerd) animal.

The owl was alive, but she was weak. The men wanted to help her. They put the injured bird in a box and drove her to a wildlife **rehabilitation** (ree-huh-bil-uh-TAY-shun) center, a special hospital for sick and injured wild animals.

Adult female spotted owls usually weigh about one and one-half pounds. The injured owl weighed just one pound—one-third less than it should have. The medical staff at the South Okanagan (oh-KAN-uh-gan) Rehab Centre for Owls force-fed the owl. She started to eat on her own, but she was still too weak to stand.

Spotted owls are birds of **prey**. They hunt for their food while in flight. The injured owl had a severe eye injury. She had been unable to see well enough to hunt for her food. Before the work crew had found her, she had been slowly starving to death.

The staff gave the owl **antibiotics** (an-tih-bye-AH-tiks) and **anti-inflammatory** (an-tih-in-FLAH-mih-tor-ee) medicine for her eye. If they could save her eye and make her strong again, they could release her into her ancient-growth forest home. Scientists call these forests *ancient* because the trees in them are at least 200 years old.

Sherri Klein founded the owl rehabilitation center. For twenty years, she had cared for sick and injured owls. This was the first spotted owl in her center. She and

Rescue workers tried to help this injured and starved one-pound spotted owl. The media attention and medical treatment by humans may have added stress to the protected bird. The owl died in their care, further reducing the number of spotted owls in the wild.

her staff gave the bird the best care they could. It was important to try to save this owl.

Although there are between 3,000 and 5,000 pairs of spotted owls throughout the world, scientists believe that as of 2008, there were only eleven spotted owls alive in British Columbia, the only area of Canada where spotted owls are found. Scientists estimate that more than 500 pairs once lived in this area. They believe that unless action is taken, the spotted owl will become **extinct** in Canada.

EXTINCTION

An owl sits high up on a tree branch in silence, watching and listening for its dinner. The nocturnal animal hunts at night, using its keen eyesight and hearing.

HUNTERS OF THE ANCIENT FORESTS

As nighttime enters the ancient-growth forest, a spotted owl **roosts** patiently on a branch. Awake all night, he searches for prey.

The **nocturnal** (nok-TUR-nal) animal's disk-shaped face remains still. Using his face as a noise funnel to catch sound, he listens intently. His small ears, hidden by feathers, can detect the faintest noise.

He sits unnoticed. His brown-and-white **camouflage** (KAA-muh-flahj) markings blend into the trees. With keen eyesight, the **predator** (PREH-duh-tur) watches for movement in nearby trees and on the forest floor. Although it is dark, the owl's large eyes let in enough light for him to see.

From as high as 100 feet, he looks for small mammals below, such as flying squirrels, pack rats, mice, and **voles**. But he'll settle for small reptiles and insects.

When he sees his prey, he spreads his four-foot-wide wings and silently swoops from his perch. His eyes track his unsuspecting dinner.

With his spread **talons** (TAA-luns), he captures his prey. The owl has no teeth, so

The wingspan of a spotted owl is the same as the height of an average seven-year-old child (48 inches). Although the human may weigh close to 50 pounds, the owl may weigh less than two pounds due to its body structure!

Spotted owls eat from a limited menu, which includes wood rats (or pack rats). They swallow flying squirrels, other small mammals, small reptiles, and even an occasional insect, whole, without chewing.

A few hours later, the owl will cough up the prey's fur and bones as a pellet. Scientists will search the forest floor for the pellets to determine what the owl ate.

he cannot chew his food. Instead, he swallows his victim whole. A few hours after ingesting his meal, the owl coughs up a **pellet**. This small egg-shaped bundle contains fur and bones—the parts he could not digest.

In the morning, he will rest. While the forest remains dark, he will search his territory for more food.

The hard outer shell of a giant centipede (SEN-tih-peed) and the whisker of a pack rat are part of this owl pellet. The size and shape of the prey's undigested bones offer scientists clues about the owl's diet.

The spotted owl is an important part of the food chain. Its diet helps to keep animal populations in balance within the ancient-forest community. Without the spotted owl, the forest could be overrun by **rodents** and flying squirrels.

Spotted owls can live for fifteen or more years in the wild. They keep the same mate for their entire life. Spotted owl parents do not build a nest each spring to raise their

owlets. They search for old nests or hollowed trees, and they may not mate every year.

The female owl lays one or two eggs in the nest. After 30 days, the eggs hatch and snowy white owlets emerge. They rely on

A female spotted owl and her two owlets anxiously watch for the male owl. The male spotted owl may catch more food than can be eaten by his young offspring. He caches (KAA-shez), or saves, the prey in tree branches for future meals.

A mature owl and an owlet rest in a broken tree stump that serves as their nest.

their parents to feed them small bites of raw meat. While the mother tends to the young owls, the father hunts.

Once a young owl has learned how to fly and hunt, it will search for an ancient-forest territory to claim as its own.

These two juvenile spotted owls are losing their white downy feathers. They will one day leave their parents' home and claim their own ancient-forest territories. They will not stay together. Instead, each owl will look for a lifetime mate.

MULTIPLE THREATS

The number of spotted owls is declining. Scientists have been watching spotted owls since the late 1800s. Wildlife **ecologist** (ee-KAH-luh-jist) R. J. Gutiérrez (goo-tee-AYR-ez) has studied spotted owl populations since 1980 to learn why their numbers are declining and how people can help protect them.

"Some [spotted owl] populations are stable," explains Gutiérrez. "The ones in Washington and some in Oregon are declining rapidly."

Other birds can be a threat to the spotted owl. As juvenile owls leave their parents' nests to search for their own territories, they may become prey for other birds. One bird that preys on the spotted owl is the northern goshawk, a type of falcon. Other spotted owls may die of starvation when they are unable to find enough food.

Spotted owls are territorial (tayr-ih-TOR-ee-ul). Except for a few months each year, when they are mating and raising their owlets, they will not share their home, or territory, with other spotted owls.

If another spotted owl, a barred owl, or an owl of any other species enters its territory, the spotted owl will leave. It rarely defends its home, but has to search for a new one. Scientists have watched barred owls as they take over spotted owl territories. This is the second threat from other birds.

Perhaps the greatest threat to the spotted owl is not another bird, however. It is people.

Spotted owls live only in ancient-growth forests. These forests provide the spotted owl with protection from predators. The forests are home to the owl's food sources. Today, there are fewer forests for spotted owls to claim as their territory. With fewer homes, there are fewer owls.

Why are there fewer homes? Old forests have old trees. These trees grow to be 100 to 200 feet tall. Their trunks are six to seven

Scientists who study animals and birds in their natural habitats are called wildlife biologists. Two owl specialists, Shawn Hilton and Vicky Young, examine a spotted owl before releasing it back into the wild.

Ancient-growth forests contain valuable trees. They also provide homes for many animals, including the spotted owl and its prey.

feet across. Old-growth forests are valuable to timber companies. Loggers remove these prized trees and send them to manufacturing plants, where they are made into building materials, furniture, and paper.

The northern spotted owl's habitat ranges from northern California to southwestern British Columbia in Canada. The logging industry has completely removed, or clear-cut, almost 70 percent of the trees from this land. The timber industry and the loggers, who take down the trees, claim they're losing money by not logging these forests. There have been bitter battles over which is more important: owls or jobs.

"Most of the trees in spotted owl habitats belong to the people of the United States and not the lumber industry," explains Gutiérrez. "It was not [the timber industry's] to begin with."

The northern spotted owl is one of three spotted owl **subspecies** (SUB-spee-sheez). It is the most threatened. The other

When people log trees, perhaps to use in the construction of houses, the forest animals must search for new homes of their own.

two subspecies are the California spotted owl, which lives only in California, and the Mexican spotted owl, which lives in Colorado and Utah and south into Mexico.

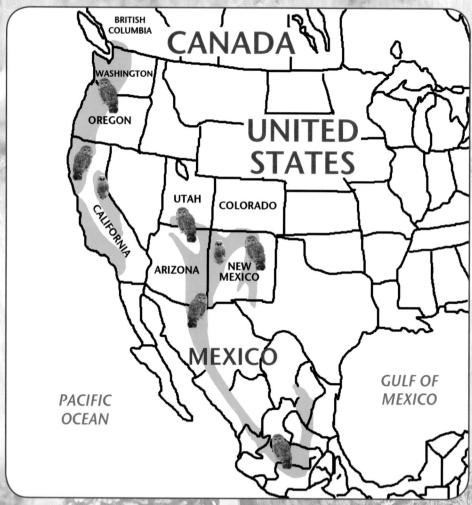

The three subspecies of spotted owls reside in western North America, from southern British Columbia, Canada, to Mexico. The spotted owl does not migrate, or fly, from one region to another.

A Mexican spotted owl is one of many species of owls. Each species has its own unique sounds or calls. The spotted owl communicates mainly with a series of four spaced notes. "Hup, hoo-hoo, hooo." It can also grunt, groan, and chatter.

Scientists are observing California spotted owls in several mountain ranges of the state. As of 2008, state officials did not consider this subspecies threatened, and in some regions of the state, the number of spotted owls has increased. The Mexican spotted owl, however, is threatened. Scientists are tracking its population carefully.

To stop logging activity, environmental (en-vye-urn-MEN-tul) activists sometimes become tree sitters. On December 10, 1997, one such activist climbed Luna, an ancient redwood tree in northern California. Julia Butterfly Hill lived upon a platform in the tree's branches for 738 days before coming down to the ground. Her tree-sit drew much media attention and awareness to the problem of logging ancient-growth forests.

SAVING THE SPOTTED OWL

The United States declared the northern spotted owl an endangered species in 1990 under the Endangered Species Act. The Mexican owl was added to the list in 1993. These owls may not be hunted or harmed.

Limited logging is allowed in areas where the spotted owl is protected. Loggers must leave enough big trees standing for the owls to nest and roost. Will it be enough to save the species?

In 2003, Canada adopted the Species at Risk Act. This law applies only to limited areas of the country and leaves the spotted owl at risk.

Scientists like R. J. Gutiérrez will continue to study these endangered animals. The more scientists know about how these birds of prey live, about their habitat, and about the impact of logging and other animals on the spotted owl's life, the more they can help the owl.

Young readers can help save the spotted owl and other endangered animals by becoming more informed. "Young readers will eventually be the people making decisions. They need to learn to think seriously about solutions to problems. They should not blindly follow [others]," suggests Gutiérrez.

In April 2006, the government of British Columbia announced a $3.4 million program to help the spotted owl recover. The program was scheduled to run for five years. Recovery efforts were to include increasing food sources for the spotted owl and limiting competing species, including the barred owl, through programs such as **capture and release**. However, many scientists believe the plan should have included more steps for protecting the owl's habitat.

A protester, dressed as a spotted owl, draws attention to the decline of this bird. Protesters use creativity and hard work to bring the owls' struggle to survive to the public's attention.

Captive breeding is also part of the proposed Canadian recovery program. Scientists plan to remove the owls from the wild. The owls will be bred in captivity, most likely in zoos. Scientists will then release the owls back into the wild. If this program is successful, scientists will release more owls than they capture. And those that are released will be trained to survive without further help from humans. The goal of the program is to break the cycle of declining spotted owl populations—but it will only work if there are forests to which the owls can return.

You don't have to sit in a tree to help save ancient-growth forests and the spotted owl. Here are a few things you can do:

Learn as much as you can about ancient-growth forests and spotted owls by reading books and magazines, exploring web sites, and attending nature programs given by wildlife specialists.

Ask your parents to purchase wood products from forests other than ancient-growth forests.

Become a young naturalist by spending time in the woods and other habitats to observe nature in action. (Be sure you go with a responsible adult.)

Contact your state representative and share your concerns.

Study hard in school. You may become a scientist who helps save endangered plant and animal species.

Visit or volunteer at a wildlife rehabilitation center to learn more about protecting our animal friends.

Ask your friends and classmates to start or participate in a wildlife conservation program.

The U.S. Fish and Wildlife Service has other recommendations for young naturalists to help conserve rare, threatened, and endangered species and their habitats. You can learn more by logging on to their web site: http://www.fws.gov/endangered/kids/kids_help.html

Books

Fitzgerald, Dawn. *Julia Butterfly Hill: Saving the Redwoods*. Brookfield, Connecticut: The Millbrook Press, 2002.

Hickman, Pamela. *Birds of Prey Rescue: Changing the Future for Endangered Wildlife*. Buffalo, New York: Firefly Books, Inc., 2006.

Lynette, Rachel. *Julia Butterfly Hill: Saving the Ancient Redwoods (Young Heroes)*. Farmington Hills, Michigan: KidHaven Press, 2007.

Martin, Patricia A. Fink. *Northern Spotted Owls (A True Book)*. New York: Children's Press, 2002.

Works Consulted

Arnold, Elizabeth. "NPR: Saving the Spotted Owl." August 5, 2004. http://www.npr.org/templates/story/story.php?storyId=3815722

"B.C. Announces Spotted Owl Recovery Action Plan." April 28, 2006. http://www2.news.gov.bc.ca/news_releases_2005-2009/2006AL0012-000514.htm

"California Spotted Owl Endangered Listing Petition Fails." http://www.ens-newswire.com/ens/may2006/2006-05-24-05.asp

"Canada's Last Wild Spotted Owls to Be Captured." http://www.ens-newswire.com/ens/may2007/2007-05-17-03.asp

"Captive Breeding Programs." http://nationalzoo.si.edu/ConservationAndScience/EndangeredSpecies/CapBreedPops/default.cfm

Chadwick, Douglas H., and Joel Sartore. *The Company We Keep: America's Endangered Species*. National Geographic Society, 1996.

Cornell University. All About Birds: Spotted Owl. http://www.birds.cornell.edu/AllAboutBirds/BirdGuide/Spotted_Owl.html

"Endangered Species Act." http://www.fws.gov/endangered/

Hill, Julia Butterfly. *The Legacy of Luna: The Story of a Tree, a Woman and the Struggle to Save the Redwoods*. New York: HarperCollins, 2000.

Interview with R. J. Gutiérrez, Professor and Gordon Gullion Endowed Chair in Forest Wildlife Research, University of Minnesota. January 12, 2008.

Interview/e-mail correspondence with wildlife photographer and biologist Jared Hobbs, June 2008.

Nagel, Robert. *Endangered Species: Arachnids, Birds, Crustaceans, Insects, and Mollusks* (Volume 2). Detroit, Michigan: Gale, 1999.

"Obit for a Spotted Owl." November 12, 2006.
http://zoeblunt.gnn.tv/blogs/19844/Obit_for_a_Spotted_Owl

Spotted Owl Biology
http://www.owling.com/Spotted_nh.htm

"Spotted Owl Fact Sheet" http://www.wildernesscommittee.org/campaigns/wildlife/spotted_owl/spotted_owl_facts

U.S. Fish and Wildlife Services: Mexican Spotted Owl
http://ecos.fws.gov/speciesProfile/
SpeciesReport.do?spcode=B074

On the Internet

Birdlife International
http://www.birdlife.org/

"Endangered Species: Kids' Corner."
http://www.fws.gov/endangered/kids/kids_help.html

Listen: The Spotted Owl
http://www.birds.cornell.edu/AllAboutBirds/audio/
Spotted_Owl.html

South Okanagan Rehab Centre for Owls
www.sorco.org

Virtual Owl Pellet Dissection
http://www.kidwings.com/
owlpellets/index.htm

Jared Hobbs releases a spotted owl in British Columbia.

GLOSSARY

antibiotics (an-tih-bye-AH-tiks)—Medicine used to slow or kill harmful germs that cause disease.

anti-inflammatory (an-tih-in-FLAH-mih-tor-ee)—Medicine used to reduce swelling.

camouflage (KAA-muh-flahj)—A disguise meant to hide.

captive breeding—Mating program used to help animals reproduce in a controlled setting.

capture and release—A program to remove animals from areas where they are not wanted and set them free in more favorable areas.

ecologist (ee-KAH-luh-jist)—A scientist who studies animals, plants, and their environments.

endangered (en-DAYN-jerd)—Threatened with extinction.

extinct (ek-STINKT)—No longer existing or present.

juvenile (JOO-veh-nyl)—Not quite an adult.

media—News sources such as newspapers, magazines, and web sites.

nocturnal (nok-TUR-nal)—Active at night.

owlet—A young owl.

pack rat (or wood rat)—A small short-tailed rodent that lives in the wild.

pellet—A bundle of fur and bones left over after an owl has digested its prey.

predator (PREH-duh-tur)—An animal that kills other animals, usually for food.

prey (PRAY)—An animal killed by another animal for food.

rehabilitation (ree-huh-bil-uh-TAY-shun)—To restore or improve to a previous level or condition.

rodent—A small, gnawing mammal, such as a mouse.

roost—To sit on a branch or support.

subspecies (SUB-spee-sheez)—A smaller group or variation of a species.

talon (TAA-lun)—The claw of a bird of prey.

tree sitter—A person who lives in a tree to draw attention to a cause.

vole—A type of small rodent, related to the muskrat.